BIOGRAPHY FROM
ANCIENT CIVILIZATIONS
LEGENDS, FOLKLORE, AND STORIES OF ANCIENT WORLDS

The Life and Times of

NOSTRADAMUS

P.O. Box
Hockessin, Delaware 19707

Titles in the Series

The Life and Times of

BIOGRAPHY FROM
ANCIENT CIVILIZATIONS
LEGENDS, FOLKLORE, AND STORIES OF ANCIENT WORLDS

The Life and Times of

NOSTRADAMUS

Russell Roberts

Printing   1   2   3   4   5   6   7   8   9

Library of Congress Cataloging-in-Publication Data

Roberts, Russell, 1953–
     The life and times of Nostradamus / by Russell Roberts.
          p. cm. — (Biography from ancient civilizations)
     Includes bibliographical references and index.
     ISBN 978-1-58415-544-7 (library bound)
     1. Nostradamus, 1503–1566—Juvenile literature. I. Title.
BF1815.N8R58 2008
133.3092—dc22
[B]
                                                                              2007023415

ABOUT THE AUTHOR: Russell Roberts has written and published nearly 40 books for adults and children on a variety of subjects, including baseball, memory power, business, New Jersey and Texas history, and travel. He has written numerous books for Mitchell Lane Publishers, including *Nathaniel Hawthorne, Thomas Jefferson, Holidays and Celebrations in Colonial America, Daniel Boone, The Lost Continent of Atlantis, Dionysus,* and *Athena.* He lives in Bordentown, New Jersey, with his family and a fat, fuzzy, and crafty calico cat named Rusti.

PHOTO CREDITS: Cover, p. 6—Superstock; pp. 1, 3—JupiterImages; p. 10—*The New York Times*; p. 12—Frederick de Wit; p. 14—*Liber Chronicarum Mundi*; p. 24—Nostradamus/Jean Brotot; 26—Jean-Loup Charmet/Photo Researchers; pp. 30, 33—Getty Images; p. 32—Time Life Pictures/Getty Images; p. 36—Paris/BnF.

PUBLISHER'S NOTE: This story is based on the author's extensive research, which he believes to be accurate. Documentation of such research is contained on page 47.
     The internet sites referenced herein were active as of the publication date. Due to the fleeting nature of some web sites, we cannot guarantee they will all be active when you are reading this book.
     To reflect current usage, we have chosen to use the secular era designations BCE ("before the common era") and CE ("of the common era") instead of the traditional designations BC ("before Christ") and AD (*anno Domini*, "in the year of the Lord").

                                                                              PPC

BIOGRAPHY FROM ANCIENT CIVILIZATIONS
LEGENDS, FOLKLORE, AND STORIES OF ANCIENT WORLDS

The Life and Times of

NOSTRADAMUS

*For Your Information

Nostradamus was many things: writer, astrologer, and physician are just some of them. In all of these pursuits the stars played an important role.

CHAPTER ONE

NOSTRADAMUS'S FINAL JOKE

Night hung like a dark cloth in the old church, smothering even the faint light from the flickering candles. A group of men gathered around a section of wall were using shovels, pickaxes, and other tools to carefully chisel out pieces of brick, stone, and other materials. They were after something that was behind the wall.

Outside the church—the Church of the Cordeliers in southern France—an owl perched on a tree branch and hooted occasionally. Its strange tones echoed, adding to the eerie atmosphere. Shadows filled the aisles where, during the day, people came to pray. The men had brought lanterns with them to provide light so that they could see while they worked, but it was almost as if the darkness were . . . alive. It seemed to swallow the light as soon as it came out of the lamps, preventing it from properly illuminating the room.

What was that? Several of the men jerked their lanterns around, swinging them back and forth as they tried to pierce the inky darkness. What had made that noise? Was it a mouse, scampering away . . . or was it something else?

Nervously the men looked around. Sweat poured down their faces, for this was hot and hard work. Their clothes were dirty and stained with perspiration. The shadows thrown off by lantern light hugged the walls, dancing and twisting as the candle flames flared up and down. Superstitious all, the men glanced around as they worked, wondering who—or what—was hiding in the darkness, ready to pounce on them.

Suddenly there was a shout. One of the workers had broken through the thick wall. Quickly he and another man began pulling more bits of brick and stone away from the edge of the hole, making the opening larger. The others crowded around, anxiously peering into the hole. What was in there?

Some of the men jumped back. Several crossed themselves and mumbled a quick prayer. Their eyes grew wide, but they could see nothing except the odd, dancing shadows on the wall. The men's nervousness increased as their eyes drifted toward the hole in the wall once again.

There, standing upright inside the wall, just past the broken pieces of brick and stone, was a coffin. It had obviously been there for many years. Spiderwebs covered it, and some of its wood was soft and rotting from water damage.

The men resumed their task, expanding the hole in the wall until it was large enough for the coffin to fit through. Carefully they reached in and pulled it out, then laid it very gently on the floor of the church. Almost as one, the entire group of men stepped back, gazing silently at the wooden box and thinking about the person it contained.

It was the coffin of Nostradamus, one of the most famous prophets in history. According to his secretary, Nostradamus had asked "not to hear feet passing over him when he slept for the last time,"[1] so his body had been entombed standing upright inside the walls of this church.

Nostradamus had died on July 2, 1566—one hundred thirty-four years before his coffin was found. All that would be left inside the coffin should be bones, a few wisps of hair, and possibly a few bits of clothing. Why, then, were the men so interested in getting the coffin out of its resting place within the church walls?

Indeed, who were these men? Were they grave robbers trying to find a secret document that was supposed to have been buried with Nostradamus? Legend said the document would explain how to interpret his famous predictions. Or were the men church officials merely trying to move the coffin of the celebrated seer to a new and better gravesite?

Napoleon Bonaparte as emperor of France, World War II, people landing on the moon, and the assassination of President John F. Kennedy. Did Nostradamus see these events occurring from his vantage point hundreds of years in the past?

No one knows. But no matter who the men were, when they opened the coffin and viewed the skeletal remains of Nostradamus, they found no document or papers that revealed the secrets of his incredible predictions. However, something they did find astonished them. For around the neck of the skeleton hung a medallion that was inscribed with the date of that very year—1700. Nostradamus had predicted the exact year in which his tomb would be broken into . . . over a century before it happened!

Quickly the men put the coffin back and resealed the tomb. No one wanted to disturb any further the remains of a man who had somehow managed to gaze through the mists of time and see so far

September 11, 2001, was the day of the worst terrorist attack on the United States in its history. Did Nostradamus peer through the mists of time and see it occurring?

into the future. How did he do it: luck, sorcery, even black magic? He was plainly not a person to be taken lightly—even in death.

Today the same thing remains true. Millions of people throughout the world are very serious about Nostradamus and his predictions, even though centuries have passed since his death. With each passing year, more and more evidence seems to indicate that Nostradamus predicted world events long before they happened. The rise and fall of Napoleon Bonaparte and Adolf Hitler . . . the French Revolution . . . wars . . . even the terrorist attacks of September 11, 2001, on New York City and Washington, D.C. People read his writings and are convinced that he predicted these occurrences. Then they turn to his other verses for even more predictions—nearly everyone wants to know the future—and Nostradamus's fame grows even greater.

Who was this mysterious Frenchman who, centuries after his death, is more popular than ever? Could he really predict the future? Did he sift through the sands of time and see things occurring 100 . . . 200 . . . even 1,000 years into the future? Should we believe him?

Tales of Nostradamus

The story in chapter 1 illustrates a major problem with investigating the life of Nostradamus. It seems that every source contains different information. Even the exact wording of his predictions are translated differently so that the same prophecy has different words! This makes it very difficult to get a clear picture of the man and his predictions.

Nostradamus lived in sixteenth-century France. Naturally there was no electronic media around to record his life. Johannes Gutenberg had only invented the movable-type printing press a few decades before Nostradamus was born in 1503.

So, without reliable sources, Nostradamus researchers often have to rely on tales about his life that may or may not be true. The story of his tomb raiders is a typical example. Did it actually happen? Did they find a medallion? No one knows. Some sources list it as a factual event, while others do not.

Here are two other stories about Nostradamus that may or may not be true, but are often presented as fact to illustrate his power of prophecy:

Nostradamus was riding along a road near the city of Ancona (right), Italy, when he came upon a group of friars (members of a religious order). He got off his horse and knelt down in front of a young friar. When asked why he was kneeling, he replied: "Because I must kneel before His Holiness"[2] (meaning the Pope) . That young friar grew up to become Pope Sextus V.

While visiting someone, Nostradamus was asked, as a test, what would be the fate of two piglets—one white, one black. Nostradamus replied that the black pig would be eaten for dinner that night, and that a wolf would eat the white one. The owner of the home quickly directed that the white pig be killed for dinner. But after the meal, an embarrassed servant replied that although he had killed the white pig as directed, a wolf had stolen it, forcing him to kill and prepare the black pig for dinner.

Are these stories true or false? No one can be certain. This ambiguity helps hide the real Nostradamus from view.

A planisphere shows what the sky will look like on a particular date and time. Nostradamus received one from his great-grandfather to read and chart the stars. The device was critical to his abilities as a prophet.

CHAPTER
TWO

AT HIS GRANDFATHER'S KNEE

The area of southern France known as St.-Rémy-de-Provence is a hilly region long known for its natural beauty. Fields of wildflowers bursting with color lie in the shadows of rugged, tree-covered mountains. Scattered around the area are the remnants of buildings erected by the ancient Romans, who lived there long ago.

The gorgeous scenery has drawn many people to it throughout the centuries, including a fair number of artists, who have tried to capture the region's picturesque charm. One of the most famous of these was the celebrated Dutch painter Vincent van Gogh, who came to St.-Rémy in the last years of his troubled life.

Long before Van Gogh arrived, however, the area was already famous for being the home of another well-known person. It was here, in a house that still stands, that Michel de Nostredame—who became known as Nostradamus—was born on December 14, 1503.

His father was Jaume (also known as Jacques or James) de Nostredame, a merchant. His mother was Reyniére (which we today pronounce and spell as Renée). In a time when poverty and hardship were common, the family lived comfortably. Originally the family name was de Gassonet, and their religion was Jewish. The area had

The Jews of Cologne [Germany] Burnt Alive, *from a 1493 woodcut. Jews across Europe had been persecuted for centuries by the time Nostradamus was born. His family thought they had found a safe place to live in southern France, but general hatred of Jews found them again.*

been a haven for Jews for years, even as many other parts of Europe were persecuting them.

However, in 1501, French King Louis XII demanded that all French citizens who were Jewish make a choice: They could either remain Jewish and have all that they owned taken away, or they could convert to Christianity. To avoid losing everything, the Gassonets changed their name to de Nostredame, a Christian name that means "Our Lady" (the Virgin Mary) in English.

When Nostradamus's father Jaume married Renée, he received a house as part of the dowry from one of her relatives, a man named Jean de Saint-Rémy. It seems likely that the house was given with the understanding that Saint-Rémy would be allowed to live there as he got older. This man, Nostradamus's maternal great-grandfather, played a major role in shaping young Michel.

Saint-Rémy had the greatest influence on his great-grandson when it came to education. Besides teaching him Latin, religion, and classical literature, the older man introduced Michel to the world of astrology.

Saint-Rémy owned a special astrological instrument called a planisphere. This was a device that, when given a certain date and time, was able to show the positions of the stars at that moment. It is known that he had this device and that Nostradamus wound up with it because Nostradamus refers to it in a letter he wrote in 1561. There is also speculation that Saint-Rémy had an astrolabe, which is a more advanced version of the planisphere.

Part of the house in which young Michel and his great-grandfather lived had no roof. Thus it was wide open to the sky. Without artificial light of any kind to hamper their view, it can be imagined that the young boy and his great-grandfather spent many evening hours in this portion of the house, gazing up at the night sky with its thousands of twinkling stars. During this time the older man likely imparted his astrological knowledge and wisdom to his great-grandson.

Saint-Rémy probably also helped Nostradamus understand all about the ancient Roman ruins that littered the area. One particularly imposing ruin that existed in Nostradamus's time (and still does) is called the Arc. It is a large stone arch that celebrates Roman General Julius Caesar's victory over a people called the Gauls. Another is a two-story mausoleum, carved with images depicting the Trojan War, gods, and sea monsters. Nostradamus and his great-grandfather probably visited the area repeatedly—the boy scampering around the ruins while the older man told him all about the glory, gods, and goddesses of ancient Greece and Rome. Nostradamus expert Ian Wilson feels that it was an easy leap for a person who grew up with a fascination for the past to also become interested in the future: "[A] mind that could become so absorbed by wandering thousands of years back into the past might well in time find a similar fascination for the future."[1]

Nostradamus, the oldest child, was soon joined by brothers and sisters. Some birth dates are unknown, and details about his siblings are sketchy or nonexistent. The first to follow him was a sister named Delphine. In 1507 a brother named Jéhan, who was to remain close with his older brother all his life, was born. Other children were Pierre, Hector, Bertrand, and another Jean. In 1522 Louis was born, followed the next year by Antoine.

Around this time, Nostradamus left his family's home to make his own way in the world. Here experts disagree on his exact path. Some feel, because of a statement by his secretary Jean-Aimé Chavigny, that he was sent to the town of Avignon in his late teens or early twenties, where he studied medicine at the University of Montpellier Medical School. Others, however, find no evidence that he began his medical studies until 1529, when he was twenty-six years old. They say that he spent the preceding five or six years traveling and learning the medical properties of plants and herbs.

Nostradamus's own words seem to support the second theory. Later in life he wrote: "I moved through a number of lands and countries from 1521 to 1529, constantly in search of the understanding and knowledge of the sources and origins of plants and other medicinal herbs."[2]

At this time there was a rivalry between those who studied to be doctors and those who practiced medicine by using plants and herbs. The doctors looked down on the herbalists because they did not have the education that doctors did; and the herbalists were resentful of the doctors for this viewpoint. Apparently Nostradamus had made some unkind comments about doctors before he enrolled at Montpellier. On October 3, 1529, there is a note next to his name by the school's proctor that Nostradamus had been removed from the student roster because of remarks he had previously made about doctors. However, whatever those remarks were must not have been too bad, for just twenty days later—on October 23—Nostradamus was back on the list of the school's medical students.

Montpellier was one of the finest medical schools in Europe. For example, even though dissections were outlawed by the Catholic Church (and France was an overwhelmingly Catholic country), a few a year were performed at Montpellier in order to gain an understanding of how the body worked. Nostradamus was also helped by the belief of the time that astrology was an important part of medicine. It was felt that each astrological sign governed a certain part of the human body. Aries the Ram was responsible for the head, Taurus the Bull controlled the neck, and so on. The star and astrological studies that Nostradamus did with his great-grandfather undoubtedly aided him.

The exact sequence of events that follows is another Nostradamus mystery. According to Chavigny, Nostradamus received his medical degree from the university. Unfortunately, the school's records do not confirm this. While their records are extensive, they are also incomplete. The typical time period for a student to receive his medical degree from Montpellier was nine years. However, the next date for which something is known about Nostradamus is around 1533 or 1534, when he was at a town called Agen in western France. This was just four or five years after his enrollment at Montpellier, and seemingly too soon for him to have obtained his medical degree. So, while it is possible for Nostradamus to have graduated from Montpellier, it cannot be stated that he did so with absolute certainty.

It seems that Nostradamus went to Agen to study medicine under a man named Jules-Cesar Scaliger. Here again lies more uncertainty. According to Chavigny, while in Agen, Nostradamus married. It is possible that his wife was Henriette d'Encausse, but again this cannot be known for sure. Nostradamus never mentioned her in his own writings. Chavigny also says that his wife bore him two children—a boy and girl. As to what their names were, official records are silent.

More mystery surrounds the next sequence of events in Nostradamus's life. His wife and children apparently died of plague while Nostradamus was away, possibly dealing with a plague outbreak in another area. If this is true, it must have been a heartbreaking time for him: He had used his medical skill to help others stricken with the plague, yet those same skills could not help save his own family.

More trouble arrived for Nostradamus when he, Scaliger, and a third man, Philibert Sarrazin, got into trouble with the Catholic Church. In the early months of 1538, official charges were brought against him that he had witnessed the making of a bronze statue of the Virgin Mary and made a disparaging remark about it. The record shows that Nostradamus was, at this time, living and working as a doctor in a village called Port-Sainte-Marie, some twelve miles west of Agen.

The charge was serious. The Catholic Church, on the defensive at this time from the rise of the Protestant religion, had unleashed the Inquisition to deal with anyone it suspected of disloyalty. Nostradamus faced a lengthy prison sentence or even death.

Thus, either from sadness over the loss of his family, or because of the charges, or even both, he left Agen, most likely sometime in the middle or later part of 1538. He was still practicing medicine, and it seems that he decided to focus on prevention and treatment of the plague.

This, then, was Nostradamus around the age of thirty-five: a man at loose ends, who had apparently lost everything, and was heading back out onto the road to ease his inner pain and to escape persecution—and hopefully to find himself again.

What he would find still echoes throughout the world.

Astrology During the Sixteenth Century

Today, astrology is something that many people regard as merely fun. Although some people do not make a move without consulting their star charts, to many, astrology is something found in the comic section of the newspaper. They read their horoscope but do not pattern their life after its predictions. However, during the time of Nostradamus, astrology was taken very seriously.

Astrologers believed that everything that happened—good or bad, past, present, or future—was spelled out in the movement and placement of the stars. According to astrologers, God's plan for a person was written in the stars. Thus, if the astrologer interpreted the stars correctly, the outcome of a person's life could be predicted. This is why the birth of a royal child prompted its parents to rush off to an astrologer, who would read the stars and tell them the baby's future.

How did a sixteenth-century astrologer do what he did? He would observe the stars with his own eyes (the telescope had not yet been invented) and write down their positions on a star chart. Then he would use mathematical formulas and devices such as an astrolabe to determine such things as the angles between constellations and the distance between planets and stars. It was an involved process requiring many charts that contained reference numbers for the astrologer.

An astrolabe

Astrologers frequently ran afoul of the Catholic Church. If the astrologer could actually determine what God had in store for someone, then he was essentially knowledgeable about God's divine plan— something that no human was supposed to know. In addition, the Church taught the doctrine of free will, which meant that people through their actions determined the course of their own lives. The Church knew that the idea of free will would be much harder to accept if people believed that their entire life was already determined by the positions of the stars.

There are many stories about Nostradamus when he was a physician— some true, some false. However, there is little doubt that he had the courage to go into plague-infested areas where few others dared go.

CHAPTER
THREE

A PHYSICIAN . . . AND MORE

What Nostradamus was doing from 1538, after he left Agen, to 1544 is unknown. However, in 1544 he was in the city of Marseilles, studying the plague and its treatment with respected doctor Louis Serre. The following year, Nostradamus's brother Jéhan became a lawyer in Aix-en-Provence, a town a bit north of Marseilles. In 1546, when the plague erupted in Aix-en-Provence with deadly fury, Jéhan desperately summoned his brother to try to help the town.

Nostradamus wrote in bone-chilling detail about what he found in Aix: "Irrespective of their ages people died even while eating and drinking. The cemeteries became so full of dead bodies that there was no more consecrated ground in which to bury them. . . . The epidemic was so violent and so evil that no one could approach nearer than five paces from victims without becoming struck down themselves. . . . Death was so sudden that fathers took no heed of their children. Many, covered in plague spots, were tossed into pits. Others were thrown out their windows."[1]

People who caught the disease were almost guaranteed to die, and they knew it. Nostradamus was deeply moved when he saw a woman with plague spots calling to him from her window. She was sewing a shroud around her body in anticipation of her death. By the time he found a chance to enter the woman's house, she was dead, inside her half-sewn shroud. She had known her fate.

Around this time, Nostradamus developed a substance for which he became famous. It was a pill made of several ingredients, most prominently crushed red roses, that he promoted as a source of plague prevention.

In the life of this controversial man, this story is one of the most controversial elements. Many sources cite Nostradamus's work among plague victims as one of the shining moments of his medical career. When he encountered a plague situation, he would have all the corpses removed. He would then prescribe unpolluted (fresh) air—in a time when it was common to shut up sickrooms. To further purify the air, Nostradamus would burn a powder of "dried rose petals, cloves, lignum aloes, iris and sweet flag roots."[2] He would also order plenty of fresh water along with his rose pills.

Did those treatments work? Did the pills work? It is hard to know exactly. It is certainly true that some of his medical practices were very modern, such as his insistence on cleanliness and personal hygiene. (Nostradamus himself bathed daily, in an age in which taking one or two baths a year was common.) These treatments removed sources of contamination, as did the removal of dead bodies. It is also unquestioned that he was a brave and dedicated doctor, going into dangerous, foul-smelling, plague-filled areas that other physicians avoided.

We know that he did, indeed, develop a rose pill, because later on he provided the recipe for it. However, as for its effect on the plague, there is uncertainty, and it will likely remain another of history's unsolved mysteries regarding his life.

Something that is not uncertain, however, is that in the year 1547, Nostradamus married for a second time. His wife was Anne Ponsarde, and the wedding occurred on November 11 in the town of Salon de

Crau, nearly 230 miles south of St.-Rémy. (Today the town is known as Salon-de-Provence.) She was wealthy, so she provided a substantial dowry to the marriage.

Even after his marriage, Nostradamus continued his journeys to other places. It was obvious that he liked to travel. Perhaps he enjoyed the camaraderie of talking with other people who made medical treatments from herbs and plants, which he did on a regular basis.

Soon, however, Nostradamus's traveling days drew to a close, and he settled down in Salon-de-Provence. He and Anne lived in a four-story house with a spiral stone staircase.

There Nostradamus began, in 1549, to publish a yearly almanac for which he became famous in his lifetime. (The one he produced in 1549 was for the year 1550, the one in 1550 for the year 1551, and so on.) At that time, an almanac was considered an indispensable publication. It contained information that was important and useful to a family throughout the year. Most almanacs contained three essential sections: an astrological guide, a calendar, and predictions of the coming year's events. These predictions were based on astrology. The more accurate an almanac's predictions, the more popular it became.

Many of Nostradamus's early almanacs were printed by Jean Brotot, who was based in the French city of Lyons. The 1555 almanac carries what is believed to be the earliest known illustration of Nostradamus. The woodcut drawing shows him sitting at a desk, writing with a quill pen. Alongside him are books on a shelf. Nostradamus has a long beard. At the time, he was fifty-one years old.

The almanacs proved popular, and Nostradamus kept producing them, sometimes even at a rate of more than one per year, for the rest of his life. But this was not his only literary endeavor around this time. In 1552 he wrote a book entitled *Treatise of Cosmetics and Jams*. It contains recipes for producing cosmetics for facial beauty, as well as recipes for making various types of jams for eating. The book was printed in 1555.

The earliest known illustration of Nostradamus appeared in his 1555 almanac.

Everything in Nostradamus's life was going quite well. He was a successful writer and enjoying growing fame, even to the point of being asked to write an inscription for a new public fountain in Salon-de-Provence. His marriage was apparently happy as well, for around 1551 he and Anne had a daughter, Madeline. On December 18, 1553, a son named César was born. Perhaps it was this peace of mind that enabled Nostradamus to write and produce a book that still shakes the world today, more than 500 years later: *Les Propheties* (*The Prophecies*).

The Black Death

Looking back from our modern perspective of miracle drugs and scientific medical treatments, it is hard to imagine how devastating an attack of plague was in sixteenth-century Europe. Typically when it struck an area, daily activity there ceased. People did not go to market, businesses closed their doors, and governments stopped functioning. The only people who worked were the grave diggers.

Parents who got sick stopped caring for their children, and kids who got sick were given up for dead. No one knew what caused the disease or why, and there was little hope for recovery. Symptoms included buboes—large swellings like gigantic blisters on the skin, particularly under the armpits or in the groin. Some were the size of eggs or apples. Accompanying the buboes was a high fever. Eventually, black spots covered a person's body.

Victims of the Black Death

When the swellings burst, blood and pus would flow forth. The stink was unbearable, and the sight revolting. Doctors were powerless against the disease, and quite often contracted it themselves from their patients.

Researchers think that the plague began in southern Russia in the 1300s, when infected rodents invaded the area. Plague then proceeded to move along trade routes, as the highly infectious disease traveled with merchants to other countries.

The Black Death cut a fearful swath of destruction through many areas. Approximately one-third of Europe's total population died during this outbreak. Some cities lost more than half their people. Some smaller towns and villages lost so many people that the town itself vanished. Although the outbreak of the 1300s ran its course by about 1352, the plague would resurface several times over the next few centuries.

Eventually physicians and town governments realized that isolating the sick was an effective way of dealing with the illness, and the plague began to disappear. Another theory given for its slackening off is that brown rats, which did not carry the disease, replaced the black rats, which did. Plague last swept through England in the 1660s, and in western Europe in the 1720s.

As Nostradamus's fame as a prophet grew, many people asked him to predict their children's future. It is doubtful whether he wore a sorcerer's hat, as he did not want to be associated with sorcery.

CHAPTER
FOUR

VISIONARY SEER, OR MIS-INTERPRETED WRITER?

Nostradamus. Predictions of the future. The two concepts are immediately linked in people's minds. There have been others throughout history who have claimed to see the future, but none are as famous—or as enduring—as Nostradamus.

Nostradamus's visions were written in a form called quatrains. These are four lines of verse that rhyme. His are undated. He called the ten chapters of his book "The Centuries," although he did not mean *centuries* in the typical sense of 100-year periods. Each of the chapters contains 100 quatrains—except for Century VII, which has just 42 because the publisher wanted to hold down the number of pages in the book. Thus there are 942 prophecies—941 rhymed and one unrhymed. (There are thousands more predictions in his almanacs, but the ones in *The Prophecies* attract most of the attention.)

How and where did he compose his visions of the future? According to how he described his method, he would go into his study late at night and seat himself on a brass tripod. (The brass tripod had three legs and a rounded, bowl-like area on which to sit.) Nostradamus would intently study a flame that came from a brass bowl filled with water, then go into something of a trance.

He wrote about his methods in the first quatrain of *The Prophecies*:

Being seated at night in secret study
Meditating alone upon the brass tripod:
A minute flame comes forth from the solitude
Making successful that which should not be believed in vain.[1]

Some experts believe that the bowl of water was filled with oils and possibly even herbs. It is possible that the herbs created an aroma that filled the air.

Next, he dipped a divining rod—a rod, typically a forked stick, that is supposed to be able to find water sources underground—into the water, and wet the hem of his robe and his foot. Then he would hear the voice of a higher being, or a spiritual entity, inside his head, and begin to write.

In the second quatrain of *The Prophecies*, Nostradamus described this procedure:

The divining wand in hand is placed in the middle of Branchus
With water he moistens the hem [of his robe] and foot
Fear! A voice quivers through his long sleeves
Divine splendour. The divine one sits near by.[2]

The Branchus to which he refers is the son of Apollo, the god of fire in Greek mythology, who also had the gift of prophecy.

This method of predicting the future has been compared with that practiced by the fabled Greek Oracle at Delphi, where priests received divine information about the future. The oracle's words were nonspecific and ambiguous, just like those of Nostradamus. They could be interpreted in many different ways—again, just like those of Nostradamus.

Nostradamus admitted that he tried to make his predictions obscure: "I have expressed everything nebulously, rather than as clear prophecy,"[3] he said. By so doing, and by not dating them, Nostradamus avoided a trap into which many of his contemporary visionaries fell. Quite often, a person who claimed visions of the future would predict that some specific, momentous event would happen on a certain day. Then, when the day passed and the event did not occur, the person was left looking silly. His credibility was reduced to zero. This was not so for Nostradamus. By deliberately leaving his predictions vague and undated, he avoided that trap. To increase the quatrains' vagueness, as well as to protect himself, Nostradamus wrote them using a mixture of French, Greek, Italian, and Latin.

Another reason Nostradamus shied away from specifics in his predictions is that he wanted to avoid being labeled as a sorcerer or some type of antireligious being. The punishment for being labeled a heretic or sorcerer was imprisonment or, most likely, death—and it didn't take much for a person to be so labeled.

So Nostradamus had to walk a fine line with his predictions. In order to maintain his credibility as a prophet, he had to be accurate . . . just not precise. He needed to write so that people could get meaning from his predictions . . . just not an exact meaning. And above all, he had to avoid offending religious authorities.

As an example of how the same quatrain can be interpreted differently, consider this one—Century I, Quatrain 3:

When the liter [litter] is overturned by the whirlwind
And faces will be covered by their cloaks,
The Republic by new men is vexed,
Then the whites and reds will judge conversely.[4]

In 1937, Henry C. Roberts, who was interpreting the Nostradamus quatrains, determined that this passage referred to the Russian Revolution of 1917. In this conflict the communist faction was known as the Reds, and their opponents were called the Whites.

Many people throughout the years have studied the life of Nostradamus and tried to determine how he made his predictions. Many people will undoubtedly continue to try, such as Henry C. Roberts (above), an authority on Nostradamus.

On the surface this seems probable. However, the Reds actually overthrew a monarchy system of government, not a republic. The lines about a liter, or litter, (which is a chair typically occupied by a royal personage and carried by numerous servants) seem to have no meaning. Finally, in 1917, the Russians did not wear cloaks.

Other Nostradamus experts have concluded that the quatrain actually refers to the French Revolution—a favorite Nostradamus topic—which began in 1789. The opposing sides were known as reds and whites, and cloaks were worn in this time period. In addition, litters were far more likely to be in use at that time.

This quatrain is just one example of how learned people can disagree significantly on Nostradamus's meanings.

Another example can be found in his references to "Hisler," such as in Century IV, Quatrain 68:

In the year very near not far from Venus,
The two greatest ones of Asia and of Africa:
They are said to have come from the Rhine and from Hisler,
Cries, tears at Malta and the Ligurian sea-coast.[5]

Some Nostradamus experts are certain that the "Hisler" referred to here and in several other places is actually Adolf Hitler, the German dictator who plunged the world into World War II. (The rest of the above quatrain is supposed to be about the early days of that war.) They say that the prophet tried to disguise Hitler's true identity by changing one letter in his last name.

Others, however, dispute those findings. They wonder why Nostradamus would have been afraid to use Hitler's real name. Since Hitler would not be born for several hundred more years, there was little for him to fear. They say the lines do not refer to Hitler at all.

Further confusing things is that, sometimes, prophecies attributed to Nostradamus were not actually written by him. This was particularly true after the terrorist attack of September 11, 2001, on the World Trade Center in New York City. The supposed words from Nostradamus are as follows:

In the City of God there will be a great thunder,
Two brothers torn apart by Chaos,
while the fortress endures, the great leader will succumb,
The third big war will begin when the big city is burning.[6]

However, although it was attributed to him as being penned in 1654, Nostradamus never wrote that quatrain. If he had, it would have been a neat trick, for he had died nearly a century earlier.

The debate rages on about Nostradamus and his prophecies. Whether they are right or wrong is a matter of personal belief and interpretation. Each person must decide for him- or herself.

In the summer of 1555, Nostradamus was summoned to the royal court in Paris by King Henri II and his queen, Catherine de Medici. He had predicted in his almanac for 1555 that the king "should watch out for himself"[7] during the month of July 1555. The queen was a big believer in astrology and predictions, so it was natural that she should ask to see him.

Nostradamus bows before Catherine de Medici, the queen of France. His fame as a prophet became so great that even royalty asked him to predict the future for them.

He arrived in Paris safely on August 15. Here is where the story of Nostradamus again takes two different paths. According to a later writing by his son César, Nostradamus was welcomed in the royal court, spoke to both the king and queen, and left, showered with gifts.

However, in a letter written by Nostradamus in 1561, he told a different story. Apparently while there, he had a mysterious visit from a woman high up in royal circles. She warned him that members of the Paris Justice Department were going to question him about his predictions. Realizing that he could be arrested and imprisoned, he immediately left Paris and returned home.

Despite his close call in Paris, Nostradamus resumed his writings. During the winter of 1555–1556, he produced two books: *The Marvellous Predictions for the Year 1557*, and an *Almanac for the Year 1557*. A few months later he wrote a third book, *The Grand New Prognostication with Portentous Predictions for the Year 1557*.

These books added to Nostradamus's ever-growing fame as a prophet. People from all walks of life began to ask Nostradamus to predict their future.

Inevitably, his rising fame brought critics. They complained that he was inaccurate, sloppy, and vague. Typical of the criticism was what another astrologer, Laurens Videl, wrote to him: "You show yourself to be so ignorant that it is impossible to find anyone to whom you are second in ignorance."[8]

The death of King Henri II of France is often cited as evidence of Nostradamus's ability as a prophet. No one today remembers that there was another who predicted misfortune for the king.

Another criticism was aimed at the people of France for believing in him: "Credulous France, what are you doing, hanging on the words of Nostradamus? . . . Don't you understand that this dirty rascal offers you only nonsense?"[9]

But, as still happens today, the attacks and criticism just made Nostradamus more popular. His books were translated into Italian, and he even traveled to Italy in 1556 to attend to publication details.

What happened next is often cited as proving Nostradamus's forecasting abilities. On June 30, 1559, King Henri II engaged in a jousting contest with Jacques de Lorges, Count of Montgomery. De Lorges's lance splintered, and the wood pieces flew with tremendous force through the narrow eye-slit of the king's golden helmet. They buried themselves in the monarch's brain just over his right eye. The king lingered in agonizing pain for a little over a week, but died on July 10.

Immediately people remembered Quatrain 35 of Century I in *The Prophecies*, which Nostradamus had written several years before:

The young lion will overcome the old one,
On the field of battle in single combat:
He will burst his eyes in a cage of gold,
Two fleets one, then to die, a cruel death.[10]

This was considered a prediction of the king's unusual death after such a freakish accident. De Lorges was younger than Henri (he was thirty, while Henri was forty), a joust was single combat between two individuals, the king wore a golden helmet, and he was blinded in his right eye. It all seemed to fit so perfectly.

Never mind that in 1556, an Italian astrologer named Luca Gaurico had warned Henri to "avoid all single combat in an enclosed place, especially near his forty-first year, for in that period of his life he was menaced by a wound in the head which might rapidly result in blindness, or even in death."[11] Gaurico had died a year earlier, and a dead prophet can't be questioned about his prediction—or make new ones. But Nostradamus was still alive—and so it was to Nostradamus that all eyes now turned.

On the Other Hand . . .

FYI
For Your Info

Just when you think you've got Nostradamus figured out—that his prophecies are vague and can be stretched to fit numerous situations—he throws in a prophecy that's so specific or contains a reference that's so exact you wonder if maybe he knew something after all. Such is the case with this verse, which is Quatrain 20 of Century IX:

At night will come through the forest of Reines
Two partners, by a roundabout way, the Queen, the white stone,
The monk-king in grey at Varennes,
The elect Capet, resulting in tempest, fire, bloody slicing.[12]

This is an almost dead-on description and explanation of the flight of King Louis XVI and his queen, Marie-Antoinette, during the French Revolution, as they tried to escape from the revolutionary mob.

On the night of June 20, 1791, the king and queen slipped out a side door of their Paris palace, got into a coach, and fled the city, hoping to reach a garrison of French troops loyal to the monarchy. They were disguised—the queen wearing a plain white dress, and the king in a gray hat and cloak. But when they stopped at the town of Varennes, they were recognized and returned to Paris. Months later the royal couple was executed by the guillotine.

Execution of Marie-Antoinette

The quatrain says that the couple will flee by night (which they did) and that the king would be disguised in gray (which he was). They apparently detoured around a forest at Reines. Most remarkably, the quatrain specifically mentions the town of Varennes—a place insignificant in history except for this one occurrence. To say that its inclusion in the quatrain is just coincidence is quite a stretch.

Nostradamus has numerous other "hits" as well, such as in prophecies that seem to accurately reference Napoleon. Even a reference to "45 degrees, fire and new city"[13] in Quatrain 97, Century VI seem a description of the events in New York City on September 11, 2001.

Did Nostradamus peer through the veil of time and foresee these events . . . and others?

Nostradamus apparently predicted that François II, like his father, would die suddenly. But even after making such unhappy predictions, he was still consulted by French royalty. Human desire to know the future is strong!

CHAPTER
FIVE

FAMOUS PROPHET

The unusual death of King Henri, and Nostradamus's apparent prediction of it, sent his reputation and popularity soaring.

On December 6, 1560, François II, the seventeen-year-old son of Henri II who had succeeded his father as king, also died unexpectedly. In his 1560 almanac (a copy of which has never been found), Nostradamus had apparently predicted for the month that a young person would lose the monarchy because of an unexpected illness.

Far away from Paris in Salon-de-Provence, in early 1561, Nostradamus was having problems. France was being swept by religious strife and violence—mobs of Catholics were attacking people they thought favored the Protestant faith—and Nostradamus was caught up in it. Despite his fame, or possibly because of it, he was accused of having anti-Catholic sympathies. The danger to him and his family was so great that they briefly fled to a town called Avignon. However, by late April 1561, Nostradamus and his family were back in Salon.

Nostradamus spent part of 1561 preparing a detailed horoscope for the young King Charles IX. In addition, he was constantly preparing horoscopes and predictions for other members of royalty, both in France and elsewhere, as well as others who wanted to know whether their future endeavors would be successful. Even churches occasionally called upon him to predict events, such as where they might find stolen articles. And, of course, he was still producing his almanacs.

Typical of the many requests he received was one from two gentlemen who wanted to know if it was all right to go hunting for gold in Spain. Nostradamus supplied them with astrological charts and directions as to where to go in Spain to find gold. His positive response to their question undoubtedly filled them with confidence that their quest would be successful. His directions proved to be wrong, but did they find gold anyway? Did they die following his directions? No one knows.

Perhaps because he was so busy and wrote quickly, which caused some to grumble about the legibility of his work, around 1561 he hired a young man named Jean-Aimé Chavigny as a secretary. Chavigny would become a key source of information about Nostradamus for future generations, yet whether or not his information is accurate or tainted by hero-worship for his employer is a matter of historical debate.

One piece of information that Chavigny did leave, however, and which is probably accurate because it seems to agree with a portrait Nostradamus had made in 1562, is a description of him around age fifty-nine. Chavigny wrote: "He was a little shorter than moderate height, physically robust, lively and vigorous. He had a wide, open forehead, a straight, regular-shaped nose and grey eyes, their expression soft though blazing when angry. . . . He was ruddy-cheeked, evident even towards old age [and had] a long, thick beard."[1]

Meanwhile, France continued to burn with religious fervor. Both sides, the Protestants and Catholics, fought one another. Gamely, Nostradamus hung on with his family at Salon-de-Provence while the countryside around him raged with violence. It wasn't until February 1563 that the troubles began calming down.

Taking advantage of the peaceful atmosphere, the Queen Mother, Catherine de Medici, and her thirteen-year-old son, Charles IX, decided to tour the country. This was no simple road trip, but a massive expedition that required a huge amount of people such as servants, cooks, tailors, and more, numbering in the hundreds, to accompany them. The gigantic group lumbered throughout France, visiting various cities. Given Nostradamus's fame and Catherine de Medici's interest in astrology and predictions, it was inevitable that the entourage would visit Salon-de-Provence. This they did in October 1564.

Without photographs, we are forced to rely on artists' renditions of how they felt Nostradamus looked. Many are accurate, but here he looks unlike the others.

Here the two royals were apparently greeted by one of Nostradamus's most astonishing prophecies: that Charles and England's Queen Elizabeth would get married sometime during 1565. Of course, as with any of his prophecies, it was all in the interpretation of the wording. As Nostradamus wrote in his almanac for 1565 (which was written in 1564): "A certain most great and supreme Virgin will be matrimonially conjoined with the Trojan blood when Saturn and Jupiter come together after no longer turning away."[2]

Queen Elizabeth was considered England's "virgin queen," while "Trojan" was Nostradamus's way of referring to France's royal family. The "no longer turning away" phrase was thought to mean that the countries of England and France, which had endured a long period of bitterness, were moving toward friendship.

This was an astounding prediction for several reasons, not the least of which was that Charles was a skinny teenager, and Elizabeth was a thirty-year-old woman. In addition, Elizabeth was expected to marry a nobleman named Robert Dudley.

Nevertheless, Charles and his mother, who were in awe of Nostradamus, considered his prediction a virtual fact. They immediately began diplomatic inquiries to determine Elizabeth's interest in such a marriage.

As a measure of how pleased the king and his mother were with Nostradamus, they gave him 200 gold crowns, and named him counselor and physician to the king—a great honor. Nostradamus wasted little time in advertising his new status as the king's doctor by putting this title on the pages of his almanac. Even though 1565 passed without the predicted marriage, it didn't seem to have any effect on Nostradamus's popularity at the French court.

By 1566, Nostradamus had other worries on his mind. His health was clearly failing. In December of 1565, he discussed his physical condition in a letter: "I became afflicted with such rheumatic pain in my hands that I was not able to supply him [a client] with his horoscope on the day that we had agreed. The pains grew worse and went from my hands to my right knee, then into my foot. It is now twenty-one days since I had a good night's sleep."[3]

Perhaps knowing that his time was running out, Nostradamus seemed to want to set the record straight. In his almanac for 1567, which he completed early in 1566, he noted that it was impossible to predict the future with any certainty. However, he also defended his work, saying that it was his duty to warn people if the stars were lining up against them.

On June 17, 1566, Nostradamus drew up his will. He left all of his considerable wealth to his wife, Anne, and their six children: Madeline, Anne, Diana, César, Charles, and André. However, he made it so that his wife would lose it all if she remarried. He did not leave anything to his loyal secretary, Chavigny.

According to Chavigny, Nostradamus and he worked quite late on the day before his death. As the secretary was leaving, Nostradamus reportedly said to him: "You will not see me alive at sunrise."[4]

The next morning, he was found dead. He was sixty-two years old. The date of his death was listed as July 2, 1566. Earlier that year, in his almanac for 1567, Nostradamus had written "a strange transmigration"[5] (journey) would occur in November 1567. Believers in Nostradamus's predictions have claimed that this was actually his way of deliberately obscuring the date of his own death (dying being its own strange journey), and is also an indication that he did somehow know when he would die.

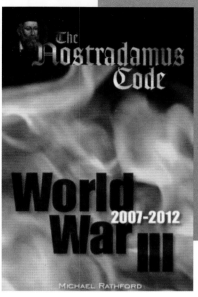

World War III is another event that some people feel Nostradamus predicted. His predictions can sometimes be used to claim that some terrible event will occur. But are his "prophecies" that specific?

While Nostradamus was indeed buried in the Church of the Cordeliers, whether or not the incident described in chapter 1 of this book actually happened is uncertain. Sometimes the story is presented as fact, and sometimes it is ignored.

But one thing is certain: Nine years before he died, Nostradamus said: "After my death my name will live on throughout the world."[6]

There can be no argument with that prediction!

FYI
For Your Info

Famous Twentieth-Century Astrologers and Psychics

Other people throughout history have claimed to be able to tell the future. Like Nostradamus, some of them used astrology for this purpose. Below are two famous astrologers, or psychics, from the twentieth century.

Jeane Dixon—Born in 1918, Jeane Dixon became famous after she supposedly predicted the assassination of President John F. Kennedy several years before it happened. Just like with Nostradamus, there are those who believe that she did and those who say she did not. Her prediction, reported in *Parade* magazine in 1956, was that a Democrat would win the 1960 presidential election, and either be assassinated or die in office, but not necessarily in his first term. (Kennedy, a Democrat, was shot in his first term.) However, she later admitted that she thought Kennedy's Republican opponent, Richard Nixon, would win the election. She also predicted that the Soviet Union would win the space race to the moon and that World War III would start in 1958.

Parade *magazine, May 13, 1956*

Joan Quigley—Just as Nostradamus enjoyed a unique relationship with French royalty, so did Joan Quigley enjoy a special relationship with the leader of another country—a United States president.

After the attempted assassination of President Ronald Reagan in 1981, Reagan's worried wife, Nancy, asked Quigley if she could have seen, and possibly prevented, the assassination attempt. When Quigley said yes, Nancy Reagan brought her into the White House as her most trusted adviser. Quigley would read the stars and advise on the feasibility of President Reagan's doing something on a certain day or time. She performed this role for as long as Reagan remained in office. Her word on the scheduling and timing of presidential moves was absolute, and no other aides, no matter how trusted, could supersede her.

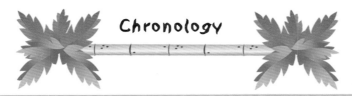

Chronology

1503	Michel de Nostredame is born on December 14 in St.-Rémy-de-Provence.
1507	His brother Jéhan is born.
1512	Michel begins education with great-grandfather Jean de Saint-Rémy.
1521–1529	He wanders the countryside learning medical properties of plants and herbs.
1522	His brother Louis is born.
1523	His brother Antoine is born.
1529	Michel enrolls at University of Montpellier Medical School.
1533–1534	He goes to Agen to study medicine with Jules-Cesar Scaliger.
1538	He leaves Agen.
1544	He studies plague in Marseilles with Louis Serre.
1546	He goes to town of Aix-en-Provence to treat plague victims.
1547	He marries Anne Ponsarde on November 11.
1549	Nostradamus begins writing yearly almanacs.
1551	His daughter Madeline is born.
1552	He writes *Treatise of Cosmetics and Jams*.
1553	His son César is born.
1555	Nostradamus writes *The Prophecies*. He is summoned to Paris to meet king and queen.
1561	He temporarily flees Salon-de-Provence for Avignon; he hires Jean-Aimé Chavigny as secretary.
1564	Nostradamus is visited by the royal family.
1566	He dies on July 2.

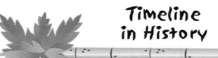

Timeline in History

1454	Johannes Gutenberg develops the printing press.
1461	The Hundred Years' War between France and England ends.
1468	The Catholic Church establishes the Inquisition.
1492	Columbus makes first voyage to New World.
1509	Henry VIII ascends to the English throne.
1512	Artist Michelangelo finishes painting the ceiling of the Sistine Chapel.
1517	Martin Luther begins the Protestant Reformation.
1520	Explorer and military leader Hernàn Cortés conquers Mexico.
1534	King Henry VIII breaks England away from the Catholic Church.
1536	John Calvin publishes first work as part of Protestant Reformation.
1541	John Calvin establishes what will come to be called Calvinism.
1543	Astronomer Nicolaus Copernicus publishes his treatise on astronomy: *On the Revolution of Heavenly Bodies*.
1558	Queen Elizabeth ascends to the English throne.
1564	Writer William Shakespeare is born.
1582	The Gregorian calendar is instituted.
1588	Spanish Armada is defeated.
1609	Galileo constructs a refracting telescope for astronomical use.

Chapter Notes

Chapter 1   Nostradamus's Final Joke
   1. Damon Wilson, *The Mammoth Book of Nostradamus and Other Prophets* (New York: Carroll & Graf Publishers, Inc., 1999), p. 103.
   2. Ibid., p. 94.

Chapter 2   At His Grandfather's Knee
   1. Ian Wilson, *Nostradamus* (New York: St. Martin's Press, 2002), p. 10.
   2. Ibid., p. 16.

Chapter 3   A Physician . . . and More
   1. Ian Wilson, *Nostradamus* (New York: St. Martin's Press, 2002), p. 46.
   2. Damon Wilson, *The Mammoth Book of Nostradamus and Other Prophets* (New York: Carroll & Graf Publishers, Inc., 1999), p. 91.

Chapter 4   Visionary Seer, or Mis-Interpreted Writer?
   1. John Hogue, *Nostradamus: The Complete Prophecies* (Rockport, Massachusetts: Element Books, 1997), p. 67.
   2. Ibid.
   3. Ian Wilson, *Nostradamus* (New York: St. Martin's Press, 2002), p. 76.
   4. Damon Wilson, *The Mammoth Book of Nostradamus and Other Prophets* (New York: Carroll & Graf Publishers, Inc., 1999), p. 97.
   5. Hogue, p. 351.
   6. Scarlett Ross, *Nostradamus for Dummies* (Hoboken, New Jersey: Wiley Publishing, Inc., 2005), p. 271.
   7. Ian Wilson, p. 85
   8. Ibid., p. 106
   9. James Randi, *The Mask of Nostradamus* (New York: Charles Scribner's Sons, 1990), p. 16.
   10. Ibid., p. 170.
   11. Ibid., p. 171.
   12. Francis X. King and Stephen Skinner, *Nostradamus* (New York: St. Martin's Press, 1994), p. 42.
   13. Ross, p. 266.

Chapter 5   Famous Prophet
   1. Ian Wilson, *Nostradamus* (New York: St. Martin's Press, 2002), p. 180.
   2. Ibid., p. 196.
   3. Ibid., p. 220.
   4. Damon Wilson, *The Mammoth Book of Nostradamus and Other Prophets* (New York: Carroll & Graf Publishers, Inc., 1999), p. 103.
   5. Scarlett Ross, *Nostradamus for Dummies* (Hoboken, New Jersey: Wiley Publishing, Inc., 2005), p. 346.
   6. Ian Wilson, p. 233.

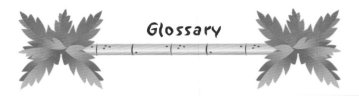

Glossary

ambiguity	(am-bih-GYOO-ih-tee)—uncertainty; being understood in more than one way.
camaraderie	(kah-mah-RAH-duh-ree)—the spirit of friendship.
disparage	(dis-PAYR-ij)—to put down; to speak badly of.
dowry	(DOW-ree)—money or property a woman brings to a man at their marriage.
endeavor	(en-DEH-vur)—to make an effort.
entity	(EN-tih-tee)—something that has an existence.
hygiene	(HY-jeen)—practices that promote health, such as keeping oneself clean.
inscribe	(in-SKRYB)—to write or engrave.
legibility	(leh-juh-BIH-lih-tee)—the ability to be read; neatness of writing.
nebulous	(NEB-yoo-lus)—cloudy, hazy, or vague.
persecute	(PUR-seh-kyoot)—to harass or cause someone to suffer because of a belief.
proctor	(PROK-ter)—a supervisor or monitor of students.
prophet	(PRAH-fit)—a person who can predict events.
quarantine	(KWAR-en-teen)—to separate from others, usually in order to keep disease from spreading.
ravage	(RAA-vij)—to attack violently and repeatedly; to destroy.
rheumatic	(roo-MAH-tik)—having swollen or painful muscles, joints, or tissue.
shroud	(SHROWD)—A cloth used to wrap a body for burial.
sorcery	(SOR-suh-ree)—showing supernatural powers, such as magic, with the aid of an evil spirit.

Further Reading

For Young Adults

Cohen, Daniel. *Prophets of Doom*. Brookfield, Connecticut: Millbrook Press, 1999.

Corrick, James A. *The Renaissance*. San Diego: Lucent Books, 1998.

Doeden, Matt. *Nostradamus*. Mankato, Minnesota: Edge Books, 2007.

January, Brendan. *Science in the Renaissance*. New York: Franklin Watts, 1999.

Obstfeld, Raymond, and Loretta Obstfeld. *The Renaissance*. San Diego: Greenhaven Press, 2002.

Peters, Stephanie True. *The Black Death*. New York: Benchmark Books, 2005.

Smoley, Richard. *The Essential Nostradamus*. New York: J.P. Tarcher/Penguin, 2006.

Tambini, Michael. *Future*. New York: DK, 2000.

Works Consulted

Hogue, John. *Nostradamus: The Complete Prophecies*. Rockport, Massachusetts: Element Books, 1997.

King, Francis X., and Stephen Skinner. *Nostradamus*. New York: St. Martin's Press, 1994.

Randi, James. *The Mask of Nostradamus*. New York: Charles Scribner's Sons, 1990.

Ross, Scarlett. *Nostradamus for Dummies*. Hoboken, New Jersey: Wiley Publishing, Inc., 2005.

Wilson, Damon. *The Mammoth Book of Nostradamus and Other Prophets*. New York: Carroll & Graf Publishers, Inc., 1999.

Wilson, Ian. *Nostradamus*. New York: St. Martin's Press, 2002.

On the Internet

Altered Dimensions: The Prophecies of Nostradamus
http://www.spartechsoftware.com/dimensions/mystical/Nostradamus.htm

Hogue, John. *Who Is Nostradamus?*
http://www.hogueprophecy.com/nostradamus.htm

Nostradamus Society of America
http://www.nostradamususa.com

Nostradamus
http://www.crystalinks.com/nostradamus.html

Nostradamus.org
http://www.nostradamus.org

Skeptic's Dictionary
http://www.skepdic.com/nostrada.html

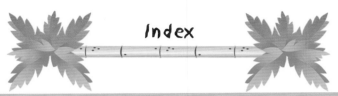

Index